Shards Of Silence

Poems of a Broken Order

Gargi Tyagi

/ BookLeaf
Publishing

India | USA | UK

Made with ❤ on the BookLeaf Publishing Platform
www.bookleafpub.in
www.bookleafpub.com

Dedication

For all who have collected the shards of life,
Yet never found the words to voice their silence.

Preface

Poetry, for me, has always been a way to hold fragments
—fragments of thoughts, moments, emotions, and
silences that refuse to fit neatly into the order of life.
Shards of Silence is a collection born from those
fragments, from the spaces between words where pain,
love, loss, and longing quietly reside.

These poems do not promise solace. They are
observations of a world both fractured and beautiful.
Some pages carry heartbreak, others carry fleeting joy;
some confront the chaos of life, while others linger in
stillness. Yet, each is a piece of a larger mosaic that
reflects the complexity of life. These poems are dedicated
to the silent moments that often go unnoticed, for the
emotions that are felt but rarely voiced, and for the
readers who may see their own unspoken truths
reflected here.

This collection does not seek to answer all questions or
heal all wounds. Instead, it invites you to sit with the
shards, to witness the fractures, and perhaps, to find
your own voice in the silence.

Gargi Tyagi

Acknowledgements

To my family and friends—thank you for your unwavering support, patience, and belief in me. Your love and encouragement have been the foundation of this collection.

We

For centuries
We were suppressed
For centuries
We were enmeshed
For centuries
We were trapped
For centuries
We were scrapped

For some
We're objects
For some
Their subjects
For some
We're insects
For some
We're the weaker sex

We still resist
All the abuse
We still subsist
Of all the dispute
Our sufferance
Seems timeless

Our refuge
Is in darkness

We're fighting
For a better reality
We're fighting
For a better mentality
We're fighting
For a better society
We're fighting
Our world's brutality

This fight
Seems endless
Our struggle
Is relentless
We may
Seem defenseless
But our strength
Is stupendous

Shakespeare's Sister

There she lays
Silent and still
No words on her lips
No words of her will

Her physical self
Never entered the world
Yet she finds herself
In every woman's word

She roamed the past
But was never seen
She'll stay till last
With the same dream

The past saw her
As dame of a mister
The future awaits her
As Shakespeare's sister

The Silent One

As I stand there in the shadows
My head weighs me down
The sounds are deafening
This dirt is my home

My legs ache and burn
Throat closing with thirst
But the fear of their sticks
Keeps me from stopping

My eyes search cautiously
My stomach rumbles and churns
Looking out for a flying stone
And scrambling for today's meal
My cries fall on deaf ears
My pain demands words
My eyes tell a story
Of a home I once had

These wounds are my blanket
As I shiver in the cold
My pain is my companion
Under this moonless sky

Sadness Sadness

The eyes search the street
Desperate for warmth
Sadness sadness
People chant
As the cold continues

The feet burn
In search of refuge
Sadness sadness
People chant
As they look down from the high

The ears long
To hear the song of salvation
Sadness sadness
People chant
As they close the door

The fear of life has now gone
The rope dangles the truth
Sadness sadness
People chant
As the spectacle concludes

The Silent Gawker

Eternally, I gawk at the span
Separate, yet marked with a blemish
Some cry out a raven
Others a storm petrel

The heavens lose color
Thunder greets the sphere
Dwellers escape the landscape
I remain, gazing still

Nothing but a banshee-critter,
They think I am free.
Few know the silence within:
Some think I'm lonely,
And some are right.

The Mother and The Men in White

They ran through open fields,
Beneath the scorching sun.
Their laughter filled the air
The world felt whole, undone.

The curious eye retreated,
Welcoming the foreign gaze.
The mother housed the strangers,
Unaware of the dark horse's ways.

They went from door to door,
Turning on their own.
Scrambling to surrender the shine,
For a master's borrowed coin.

They carried loaded rifles,
With pain's bright flame within.
The mother cried in silence,
Stained by her children's sin.

The ambushed flames rekindled,
The land began to rise.
The men in white declared,

And the dark took new disguise.

The fire they lit kept burning,
And caught her woven clothes.
She watched her waters redden
The wound the empire chose.

Her children still kept fighting,
The mother still kept crying.
While gold ships sailed away,
And left her broken, dying.

Miles Away

The moon appears full and bright
Even as it sits miles away
Its glow never diminishes
Even as it sits miles away

It lightens the dark sky
Even as it sits miles away
The moon embraces me
Even as it sits miles away

Your Light, Borrowed and Becoming

As my pain takes on a new form
The sweetness seems more
The wait is ever stretching
But not daunting anymore

Though I long to meet you
Life is not bleak anymore
The moon shows me your light
And I'm not alone anymore

Like a Child's Would

As I look at the sky
The white swirls with the blue
My eyes widen
Like a child's would

As I look at the people
Some milling, some giddy
My heart swells
Like a child's would

As I look at the flowers
Butterflies dance around
My body moves
Like a child's would

As I wake up cold
Reality grips me
My lips cry out
Like a child's would

The Season Within

I can feel the winter approaching
But mine never left
I can feel the summer slipping
But mine never came
I can see the spring in other grounds
But my toil never flowered
I can see the butterflies dancing
But my heart is cold

Mother

Even though I am a mother,
My feet still ache for shelter.
Even though I am a mother,
My mouth still longs for a morsel.
Even though I am a mother,
My pain goes unobserved.
Even though I am a mother,
I'm only worshipped in shrines, in words.

The Sky Between

The clouds glide away,
Leaving the sky empty.
Where the moon once reigned
Shines the sun's first ray.

A Morsel

Here and there
I search for a morsel
One home to next
I search for a morsel
One face to next
I search for a morsel
Yesterday and today
I search for a morsel

Found a stone and a stick
But never a morsel
Tasted pain and hunger
But never a morsel
Got screams and abuses
But never a morsel
Days came and nights
But never a morsel

The Same Light

I saw them dancing in the sky
Could be tears, could be stars.
My eyes see both the same,
For both are born of my heart.

The Raven's Calm

Whether it's death or life,
The raven cries the same.
Whether it's storm or silence,
The raven flies the same.
Whether it's pain or solace,
The raven sleeps the same.
Whether it's end or start,
The raven looks the same.

Blood Moon

Longed for you so much,
The moon bled red
Mirroring my broken heart,
Drowned in the dark of your absence.

The Dance of Life

In the dance of life
Every memory is a beat
Every word is a step
Every laugh is a melody

In the dance of life
Every person is a song
Every minute is a new note
Every breath is a reminder

In the dance of life
Every pain is remembered
Every smile is cherished
Every moment is fleeting

In the dance of life
Every page is turned
Every chapter is read
Every book is shelved

Behind the Smile

A smile can either show the brightest of joys
Or hide the darkest of scars
Every eye passes a new judgement
Yet the truth remains blindfolded

No Humans Left

The streets disappear beneath feet
But there are no humans left
The air rings with voices
But there are no humans left

Windows waft the smell of food
But there are no humans left
Every new building touches the sky
But there are no humans left

Stars appear closer to the eye
But there are no humans left
Halls fill with dancing silks
But there are no humans left

Helpless eyes look up from dirt
But there are no humans left
Screams echo in the night's silence
But there are no humans left

The Lost Realm

The city hums in static dreams
Silence reigns where eyes once spoke
We built bridges from steel
And forgot the ones built from love

The Quiet Ones

They walk in perfect lines
Heads bowed to glowing suns
No one minds the growing silence
The world forgot to listen
A bird sings sweet songs
A child laughs merrily
But all that echoes back is solitude
As the glowing sun grows stronger

A cold hand reaches out
But the glowing sun burns it
Time races past the bowed heads
But no one stops to notice

The glowing sun slowly multiplies
Surrounding the tied minds
As the bowed heads finally look up
All they see is the bright light

www.ingramcontent.com/pod-product-compliance
Lightning Source LLC
Chambersburg PA
CBHW051002030426
42339CB00007B/444